Get the Life YOU Want
FOCUS Workbook & Journal

Monica Belcher
Charlene Nelson

WriteHouse Publishing
Washington, DC

Copyright © 2012 by Monica Belcher & Charlene Nelson

All Rights Reserved. No part of this book may be used or reproduced in any manner whatsoever without written permission, except in the case of brief quotations in critical articles or reviews. For information: contact WriteHouse Publishing/BFC, LLC – www.buildforwardcoaching.com

Printed in the United States of America

ISBN-13: 978-1479309115
ISBN-10: 1479309117
Library of Congress Number: 2011962404(2)

1. Business
2. Education
3. Personal Development
4. Self-Improvement

Cover designed by **Colin Nchako**
Logo designed by William Maxwell

Kudos to Sheri Betts for being the first reader to suggest creating a journal-type offering to complement **'Get the Life YOU Want! 52 Guaranteed Success Strategies.'**

BUILD FORWARD COACHING

FOCUS WORKBOOK & JOURNAL

CONTENTS

Thank You So Much!	1
What You Gain / Use Effectively	3
FOCUS	5

F – FIND WHO/WHERE YOU ARE FIRST

1. R. U. N. There	9
2. Let It Go	13
3. Selfishness is a Monster	17
4. Do NOT Pursue a Mirage	21
5. When the Fog Lifts	25
6. Own Up To It	29
7. The Truth Brings Responsibility	33
8. Are You Really That Good	37
9. Harsh Treatment or Building Genius	41
10. You Can't Drag an Elephant	45
11. The Domino Effect	49
12. Y Go It Alone	53
▶ Your Focus – Strategy – Timeline	57

v

FOCUS WORKBOOK & JOURNAL

O – OWN EVERY OPPORTUNITY

13. How Are You Getting There	61
14. Don't Discount It	65
15. Procrastination	69
16. 25 Seconds	73
17. Thirteen Inch Screen	77
18. Confidence is Worth its Weight in Gold	81
19. (*Don't Bring* Your Present Situation Into) Your New Opportunity	85
20. Challenge Accepted	89
21. Make It Happen	93
22. Show Up…TODAY	97
23. Be Professional	101
▶ Your Focus – Strategy – Timeline	105

C – Courage, Creativity, Caring = A winning combination

24. It's In There	109
25. Strength to Speak	113
26. Start BELIEVING	117
27. Give It Time Please	121
28. Connecting the Dots	123
29. Lysol or Scrubbing Bubbles	127
30. Change Direction	131
31. Make It Happen II (Gut It Out)	135
32. Be Flexible	139
33. Is It Real or Not	143
▶ Your Focus – Strategy – Timeline	145

U – YOU REALLY DO MATTER

34. Here's to You	149
35. Not Perfection but Progress	153
36. Relationship Practices *(That Really Work)*	157
37. The Ever Evolving You	161
38. Chaos Needs No Accommodation	165
39. You Eat With Your Eyes First	169
40. The Difference Maker	171
41. Investment Translates to Ownership	175
42. A Heart to Come Home To	179
▶ Your Focus – Strategy – Timeline	183

FOCUS WORKBOOK & JOURNAL

S – SUCCESS AS A WAY OF LIFE

43. A Good Loss	187
44. Do a Good Day's Work *and* Act Like Somebody	191
45. Only the Best Will Do	195
46. Unmistakably You	199
47. Play Your Game	203
48. Can You Recognize It	207
49. Leadership	211
50. Sharpened Image, Refined Goods	215
51. Pass It On	219
52. Wow, Keep It Coming	223
▶ Your Focus – Strategy – Timeline	225

FOCUS WORKBOOK & JOURNAL

Thank You So Much!

When we wrote 'Get the Life YOU Want: 52 Guaranteed Success Strategies' we had high expectations, however, nothing could've prepared us for the outrageously wonderful responses from around the globe. Your emails, calls, letters, tweets, reviews and messages have spoken to us in a profound way. Even more than these amazing responses, Monica and I agree the VERY best response is when we get to witness the result of someone who has invested to the point of implementing our FOCUS format and then seeing their life being transformed...strategy-by-strategy! What an absolute joy! We're incredibly grateful because we were the first partakers and live the FOCUS format everyday. We celebrate all who inhale the sweetness of true fulfillment in their lives!

Yet, many of you asked for more. Along with our tenacious efforts, (coaching & training), we challenged ourselves to find a creative means to accommodate the *volume* of need 'Get the Life YOU Want: 52 Guaranteed Success Strategies' has awakened. Our emphasis for *consistent* success is straightforward – interactive participation and full commitment in putting each strategy to *work*. The **FOCUS WORKBOOK & JOURNAL** is the optimal tool in getting maximum results to attain the quality life you deserve.

FOCUS WORKBOOK & JOURNAL

What You Gain:

In 'Get the Life YOU Want: **FOCUS WORKBOOK & JOURNAL**' you'll learn to:

1) **Design Your FOCUS Points**
2) **Create Your Personal STRATEGY**
3) **Execute Your DOABLE Timeline(s)**
4) **JOURNAL with life-grafting Success**

You'll enjoy this excursion and gain strength knowing you now have a plan in place.

How to Use *Most Effectively*:

- **Be Honest**

- **Stay Focused**

- **Work it the way it works BEST for you** (Use it *with* **'Get the Life YOU Want: 52 Guaranteed Success Strategies.'** You can start from the beginning or lock in on the strategy you need to implement more readily)

- **Journal** (this will serve you as a productive exercise that greatly benefits your understanding, evolvement and personal reference)

- **Pursue/Plan/Pace** (your purpose/with relevant goals/yourself realistically)

- **Have Expectation** (for each strategy to provoke genuine change, challenge yourself to grow and to experience the continuity of successful living)
- **Walk the Strategy out in your day-to-day** (*practical* application has a lasting imprint)

- **Have Fun** and **Live out loud** (nothing should have you dancing like the nearness of being able to Get the Life YOU Want)

- **Share** (what you gain, learn and develop with someone you care about)

- **Keep your QUALITY Life intact** (by using the WORKBOOK & JOURNAL to maintain your FOCUS and keep your edge alive)

- **GET THE LIFE YOU WANT!** (no more need be said…Let's get right to it)

FOCUS WORKBOOK & JOURNAL

FOCUS

F	▶	Find who/where you are first
O	▶	Own every opportunity
C	▶	Courage, creativity, caring = a winning combination
U	▶	U *really* do matter
S	▶	Success as a way of life

"Strategies come through rough terrains you're able to navigate successfully; use them wisely and to your good."
 - Dr. Charlene Nelson

FOCUS WORKBOOK & JOURNAL

FOCUS

FIND WHO/WHERE YOU ARE FIRST

Guaranteed Success Strategy #1
R.U.N. There

1. Unexpected setbacks and trauma affect us in differing ways. How have you responded to the situations that could've been major hindrances in your life?

When I am faced with situations in my life I shut down. I block anything, anyone, who has the potential to cause anymore "setbacks." I take this time to reflect: causes, effects, solutions, and outcomes.

2. How have you learned to live with, through and after difficult situations?

If it is possible for me to solve the problem, I try. If not I avoid. Try to live day by day and keep moving. After a situation has past I try not to think about it. Make sure it doesn't happen again.

3. Assess your survival -- have you grown in character or dwarfed into mediocrity?

Dwarfed into mediocrity. (Just talking to a friend about this today). "We are what we eat." My fault for putting it in my mouth.

4. Do you have the internal tools to rebound from any situation? List what are they?

I say I rebound pretty well. Some situations take longer than others. Usually, avoidance works for me. Analyzing. Prayer.

JOURNAL

Get the Life YOU Want and the FOCUS YOU need by journaling.

Get the most out of your workbook. Write down your thoughts, insights, feelings, struggles, ideas, dreams, new concepts, plans/goals or anything that assists you.

Usually, I am able to journal on end, but lately I haven't been motivated to. Mostly I've been stuck in a never ending cycle of thinking. Often I think of nothing of substance, although, sometimes I let something slip through the cracks of my wild imagination: Serious things, crazy new ideas, controversial ways of thinking. You name it I think in. Wish I could shut my brain off for just a second.

Guaranteed Success Strategy #2
Let It Go

1. When evaluating particular occurrences and events that have happened in your life it's necessary to do so with *objectivity*. When you extract from those objectives, what stands out to you?

In life, things are always changing. If I'm thinking objectively, the first thing I like to ask myself is "if I change with the new season, who will I be?" And if I do change, will I be better or worse.

2. In your objectivity, you categorize what was accomplished and what wasn't. What's the plan for using that information to benefit your future?

In thinking categorically, first I make it known to myself that plans are not set in stone. I don't get my hopes up for the future, but if I let myself dream, I align my first steps to benefit me 5 steps down the line.

3. Often fear of history repeating itself paralyzes us from venturing past our comfort zone to have new and rewarding experiences. If you've been fearful, what's your approach in beating that fear?

I do what makes me uncomfortable in situations like those. Why not? What else do I have to lose.

4. Not being held prisoner to negative or positive life happenings frees us to have new experiences. When the events are positive they too can keep us locked into familiar patterns. How do you plan to 'let go' of the familiar in order to venture into areas that are different and diverse?

In order to let go of familiar patterns and venture out I take comfort in knowing that, "what doesn't kill me makes me stronger. Also, I love challenges so if it looks impossible it is in me to have to try; even if a part of me doesn't want to.

JOURNAL

Get the Life YOU Want and the FOCUS YOU need by journaling.

Get the most out of your workbook. Write down your thoughts, insights, feelings, struggles, ideas, dreams, new concepts, plans/goals or anything that assists you.

_____

_____

_____

_____

_____

_____

_____

_____

_____

_____

_____

_____

_____

_____

_____

_____

Guaranteed Success Strategy #3
Selfishness is a Monster

1. What events have taken place in your life that you no longer think in terms of *giving* but now in terms of receiving?

   My time is my own. Things that hold monetary value are irrelevant. Things I hold dear and somewhat selfishly are things that can't be or are not easy to get back: time, trust, respect, etc.

2. While your selfishness may not be immediately obvious to others, at your core *you know* it's all about you. If you've become a self-centered monster; what has shut down inside that you're comfortable with how you've become?

   Letting one to many people see me as a punk. I have no choice but to "get mine". If you are along for the metephorical ride then come on, but if not I don't have time.

3. How do you *change* the selfishness that you've recognized in you?

Baby steps. Noticing the small acts of selfishness and starting there.

4. There's a balance between making sure you're straight and being thoughtful of others. How do you plan on maintaining that balance?

Being more aware.

5. Often a better world comes by sharing one small act of kindness. What was your last act of kindness and to whom?

Every Friday, when I get paid, I put atleast $20 in my moms piggy bank ... she has no clue.

JOURNAL

Get the Life YOU Want and the FOCUS YOU need by journaling.

Get the most out of your workbook. Write down your thoughts, insights, feelings, struggles, ideas, dreams, new concepts, plans/goals or anything that assists you.

- I need to work on ways to take out frustration & anger
- I need to figure out my next step because where I'm at isn't it.

Guaranteed Success Strategy #4
Do NOT Pursue a Mirage

1. Is there a struggle in you to be someone or something that you're not made-up to be? Explain your journey to self-realization?

I guess we all have that struggle. My struggle comes with experimentation. I have boundaries but they are skewed dependent on my mood. I don't know an exact point of realization. High school maybe? I has gotten me into trouble, especially with drugs.

2. Do you love who you are? Do you love what you do? What makes you love it or what keeps you from loving it?

No I don't love who I am. I can't love what I don't understand. I don't understand me. As for what I do, I love my job. I enjoy my social life, but I don't love the lifestyle.

3. From your experiences what would you say to those who have pursued something misleading, deceptive or unattainable?

Run as fast as you can. It isn't worth the pain.

4. What is your understanding of 'finding your calling?'

I know I have this craving to help, even when I don't want to. My empathy level is through the roof (I hate that). Other than that, nothing.

5. How do you know when you've found that 'real YOU?'

Neon lights I guess. I haven't found me yet.

JOURNAL

Get the Life YOU Want and the FOCUS YOU need by journaling.

Get the most out of your workbook. Write down your thoughts, insights, feelings, struggles, ideas, dreams, new concepts, plans/goals or anything that assists you.

The last few weeks I have been struggling to keep my emotions in check. I've been jumping to anger more readily. The more people I'm around the madder I get.

I hate it when you think you have something figured out and then it slaps you in the face. Just been thinking alot about what I did wrong. I feel deeply sorry and I don't know why. Just have to fix it some how. Fix me.

Guaranteed Success Strategy #5
When the Fog Lifts

1. Hazardous foggy conditions in your mind can lead to doing and saying things you regret and wish you could undo. Experience teaches us to wait; to avoid regrets. What methods have you employed to make sure you don't do things you regret?

Usually if I have a thought that I may regret something, I don't do it. Although, usually if I don't do something because I may regret it then I regret that I didn't do it. If that makes any sense?

2. When you're in a holding pattern, electing not to move or make decisions until a more opportune time is crucial. How do keep your focus in that interim time?

I meditate my way through it. I get lost in thought. Somehow, everything always works itself out in patience.

3. Often revisiting a situation allows a better perspective. Have you found occasion to pull an old idea up and tweak it? Was it a part of the answer you were looking for? Explain.

If I have I can't think of one.

4. Map out your approach to dealing with a difficult and seemingly impossible situation; how do you / will you handle it?

I wait and explore my options. Almost always there is another way. I have never been stuck in a situation that there wasn't a way out of. I may have felt that way at the time, but never for long!

JOURNAL

Get the Life YOU Want and the FOCUS YOU need by journaling.

Get the most out of your workbook. Write down your thoughts, insights, feelings, struggles, ideas, dreams, new concepts, plans/goals or anything that assists you.

- Jackie came back a few weeks ago.

- Uncle died Saturday. (Herbie)

- Joined a Basketball team.

- Trying to quit smoking... again.

Guaranteed Success Strategy #6
Own Up To It

1. As a generally responsible person, what jars you when you're acting in an irresponsible way?

I like the challenge of testing my own strength. In every way possible in life I am my biggest cheer leader and my biggest self sabotage. If there is a risk I am there.

2. Was there difficulty in acknowledging the behavior that you were not proud of? Explain.

Owning up to doing wrong has never been a problem for me. But pride does get in my way to the point where, I know I'm wrong, say I'm wrong, but still do wrong. Don't know why, guess it is part of this game I play.

3. Has your level of self-respect changed one way or the other based on your behavior? Explain.

Yes, I'd be an idiot if I said no. If I am walking in a season of self-respect I'm a little more reserved, but open. If I'm not then I'm more out going but cold.

4. With a fresh awareness, what does 'acting responsibly' now mean to you?

Doing what I know needs to be done rather that doing what I want.

5. What's your process for 'doing the right thing?

Is there a process? You do it...

JOURNAL

Get the Life YOU Want and the FOCUS YOU need by journaling.

Get the most out of your workbook. Write down your thoughts, insights, feelings, struggles, ideas, dreams, new concepts, plans/goals or anything that assists you.

I remember the day I learned what exactly a risk was. I was maybe in second or third grade. It was a lesson in class: "risks and benefits". I was so interested. It was then that I started to recognize a little bit of how the world worked. That sacrifice is neccessary for growth.

Guaranteed Success Strategy #7
Truth Brings Responsibility

1. How do you define truth?

2. In our efforts to be diplomatic, and politically correct we sometimes skirt the truth, dress it up or even water it down. How do you handle dealing with the truth on a daily basis?

3. Does it frighten you to see things for what they really are? Yes or No, explain.

_____

_____

_____

_____

_____

4. Is it better to avoid the truth for a pretense of peace or face if not really knowing the liability? Explain.

_____

_____

_____

_____

_____

JOURNAL

Get the Life YOU Want and the FOCUS YOU need by journaling.

Get the most out of your workbook. Write down your thoughts, insights, feelings, struggles, ideas, dreams, new concepts, plans/goals or anything that assists you.

_____

_____

_____

_____

_____

_____

_____

_____

_____

_____

_____

_____

_____

_____

Guaranteed Success Strategy #8
Are You Really That Good?

1. There's always more in us to give so that we can be better than who we presently are; what's your plan in realizing the improved person that lies inside of you?

   _____
   _____
   _____
   _____
   _____

2. Do you find honesty in the accolades others give you or do you find them exaggerated? How close are you to the truth of what they say?

   _____
   _____
   _____
   _____
   _____

3. Everyone needs someone in their life they respect who will only speak the truth about who they are. What would it mean to you to have that complete kind of honesty coming from someone who only wants what's best for you?

_____

_____

_____

_____

_____

4. Criticism is not just disapproval, it is accurate analysis, i.e., it examines. With accurate critique, analyze yourself from the standpoint of how you're using your abilities and capabilities.

_____

_____

_____

_____

_____

JOURNAL

Get the Life YOU Want and the FOCUS YOU need by journaling.

Get the most out of your workbook. Write down your thoughts, insights, feelings, struggles, ideas, dreams, new concepts, plans/goals or anything that assists you.

Guaranteed Success Strategy #9
Harsh Treatment or Building Genius

1. How involved are you in the lives of the children/young people in your life?

   _____

   _____

   _____

   _____

   _____

2. If you had active giving, caring and sharing adults during your years of growth and development, how has that helped make you who you are?

   _____

   _____

   _____

   _____

   _____

3. So much of today's perversion and callousness comes from a lack of guidance. Describe the 'difference maker' in your life and what they actually did to make an impression on you?

_____

_____

_____

_____

_____

4. Being cool and letting our children find their way is viewed as allowing them to explore their freedom and liberties. Is that how you see it, why?

_____

_____

_____

_____

_____

JOURNAL

Get the Life YOU Want and the FOCUS YOU need by journaling.

Get the most out of your workbook. Write down your thoughts, insights, feelings, struggles, ideas, dreams, new concepts, plans/goals or anything that assists you.

Guaranteed Success Strategy #10:
You Can't Drag an Elephant

1. What's your position when you know you can't help someone whose course of action will surely lead to a very unfavorable and undesirable end?

　

2. How long does it take for you to realize someone you're trying to help really doesn't want what you're offering?

3. Do you have an internal check to keep you from wasting your efforts or becoming entangled with undue frustration?

_____

_____

_____

_____

_____

4. How has your caring and listening skills increased?

_____

_____

_____

_____

_____

JOURNAL

Get the Life YOU Want and the FOCUS YOU need by journaling.

Get the most out of your workbook. Write down your thoughts, insights, feelings, struggles, ideas, dreams, new concepts, plans/goals or anything that assists you.

Guaranteed Success Strategy #11:
The Domino Effect

1. Understanding the difference between affect and effect, domino's have to be set-up very close in proximity to **effect** each other. Who is close enough to you for you to be **affected**?

_____

_____

_____

_____

2. Are you affected in a positive or negative way? Explain.

_____

_____

_____

_____

3. Explain whether your closeness is by design or default?

_____
_____
_____
_____

4. Are you connected to people that bring like values to the equation or is there disparity? (Is it from you or them)?

_____
_____
_____
_____

5. Explain whether or not your values are enhanced, compromised or do they remain the same as a result of your associations?

_____
_____
_____
_____

JOURNAL

Get the Life YOU Want and the FOCUS YOU need by journaling.

Get the most out of your workbook. Write down your thoughts, insights, feelings, struggles, ideas, dreams, new concepts, plans/goals or anything that assists you.

Guaranteed Success Strategy #12:
Y Go It Alone!?!

1. Do you consider yourself a loner? Why is that?

   _____

   _____

   _____

   _____

   _____

2. Do you find being with or working with others a disadvantage to you? Explain.

   _____

   _____

   _____

   _____

   _____

3. Have past experiences led you to this place of feeling better off by yourself or does your personality seem to clash with associations and collaborations?

_____
_____
_____
_____
_____

4. If things could work out differently would you take the opportunity to share yourself with others, explain?

_____
_____
_____
_____
_____

5. If you want to come out of a loner mentality, what's the plan for change?

_____
_____
_____
_____
_____

JOURNAL

Get the Life YOU Want and the FOCUS YOU need by journaling.

Get the most out of your workbook. Write down your thoughts, insights, feelings, struggles, ideas, dreams, new concepts, plans/goals or anything that assists you.

Now Work YOUR Plan:

| F | ▶ | **Find who/where you are first** |

    A.   **FOCUS POINTS**

            _____

            _____

            _____

            _____

    B.   **CREATE YOUR STRATEGY**

            _____

            _____

            _____

            _____

    C.   **YOUR SPECIFIC 'DOABLE' TIMELINE**

            _____

            _____

            _____

            _____

FOCUS Workbook & Journal

fOcus

Own Every Opportunity

Guaranteed Success Strategy #13:
How Are You Getting There?

1. You have dreams and goals. They take discipline, perseverance and planning. What kind of roadmap have you laid to reach those dreams and goals?

   _____

   _____

   _____

   _____

2. Your aspirations may be a total 180 degrees from where you are now. Have you met with discouragement, rejection or disapproval to reach your desired destination? Explain.

   _____

   _____

   _____

   _____

3. It takes more than talking and planning; it takes doing. What have you *done* since you've last talked about it to prove your determination?

_____

_____

_____

_____

_____

4. Setting goals along the way makes it more manageable and less daunting. What 'doable' goals have you set?

_____

_____

_____

_____

_____

JOURNAL

Get the Life YOU Want and the FOCUS YOU need by journaling.

Get the most out of your workbook. Write down your thoughts, insights, feelings, struggles, ideas, dreams, new concepts, plans/goals or anything that assists you.

Guaranteed Success Strategy #14:
Don't Discount It

1. Do you have a system in place that you recognize as a belief system?

   _____

   _____

   _____

   _____

   _____

2. What dynamic does your belief bring to your daily planning and preparation?

   _____

   _____

   _____

   _____

   _____

3. How do you recognize the belief working beyond you that factor into the accomplishments and achievements you've attained?

_____

_____

_____

_____

_____

4. Has your experience and maturity brought you to the point that you readily acknowledge the beliefs that have impacted your life? How?

_____

_____

_____

_____

_____

JOURNAL

Get the Life YOU Want and the FOCUS YOU need by journaling.

Get the most out of your workbook. Write down your thoughts, insights, feelings, struggles, ideas, dreams, new concepts, plans/goals or anything that assists you.

_____

_____

_____

_____

_____

_____

_____

_____

_____

_____

_____

_____

_____

_____

_____

_____

Guaranteed Success Strategy #15:
<u>Procrastination</u>

1. Procrastinators are people who are professional wasters. Do you find yourself making exceptions for yourself or for those you love when they don't come through at the agreed upon time? Explain why that keeps happening?

   _____
   _____
   _____
   _____

2. Why do you rationalize putting things off that should have already been accomplished?

   _____
   _____
   _____
   _____

3. Why keeps you from doing what needs to be done?

_____
_____
_____
_____

4. Name an important opportunity you've lost because of your delay?

_____
_____
_____
_____

5. What practices do you need to put in place so you won't become a lifelong procrastinator?

_____
_____
_____
_____

JOURNAL

Get the Life YOU Want and the FOCUS YOU need by journaling.

Get the most out of your workbook. Write down your thoughts, insights, feelings, struggles, ideas, dreams, new concepts, plans/goals or anything that assists you.

Guaranteed Success Strategy #16:
25 Seconds

Consider the time and effort it's taken for you to be the person you are and accomplish the things you've accomplished.

1. There certainly have been situations in which you could've easily yielded to the irritation and frustration you were feeling. What kept you from succumbing to what you were experiencing?

   _____
   _____
   _____
   _____
   _____

2. If you were overwhelmed and gave way to that over the top moment, in hindsight, what have you learned that will keep you from going there again?

   _____
   _____
   _____
   _____
   _____

3. Sometimes there are unrecoverable moments. How do you adjust from them?

4. What would you say to someone who is paying dearly for a grave misuse of 25 seconds of their life?

JOURNAL

Get the Life YOU Want and the FOCUS YOU need by journaling.

Get the most out of your workbook. Write down your thoughts, insights, feelings, struggles, ideas, dreams, new concepts, plans/goals or anything that assists you.

Guaranteed Success Strategy #17:
Thirteen Inch Screen

1. In an opinionated society, what kind of realities have you come to that have been eye openers of how limited your views have been?

   _____
   _____
   _____
   _____
   _____

2. Have those eye openers affected the way you approach things? How so?

   _____
   _____
   _____
   _____
   _____

3. Some of our political rightness can go against everything you believe and stand for. How have you been able to demonstrate kindness and friendliness to others that go completely against your grain?

_____

_____

_____

_____

_____

4. Do your 'ah-hah' moments play out where you once were limited?

_____

_____

_____

_____

_____

JOURNAL

Get the Life YOU Want and the FOCUS YOU need by journaling.

Get the most out of your workbook. Write down your thoughts, insights, feelings, struggles, ideas, dreams, new concepts, plans/goals or anything that assists you.

Guaranteed Success Strategy #18:
Confidence is It's Weight in Gold

1. How would you gauge your confidence level?

2. Having self-worth, self-esteem and confidence in your abilities is something that happens over the course of time. Can you pinpoint what brought you to the place of realizing your value?

3. What kind of network of efficiency and success have you been able to build as a result of your confidence level being established?

_____

_____

_____

_____

_____

4. Experience is a *sure* teacher. From what you've learned, what would you be able to pass on to others?

_____

_____

_____

_____

_____

JOURNAL

Get the Life YOU Want and the FOCUS YOU need by journaling.

Get the most out of your workbook. Write down your thoughts, insights, feelings, struggles, ideas, dreams, new concepts, plans/goals or anything that assists you.

Guaranteed Success Strategy #19:
(Don't Bring **Your Present Situation into)**
Your New Opportunity

1. Are you now or have you been in a state of stagnation? What held you in that position?

2. What is it that shackles your feet, cuffs your hands, and has your mind under arrest not allowing you to be fully engaged in this new opportunity?

3. "Your present state of affairs cannot be allowed to overshadow the endless landscape you're about to embark on." How do you make sure it doesn't?

4. What is your understanding of the statement? **"Every opportunity holds the possibility to everything that means anything to you."**

JOURNAL

Get the Life YOU Want and the FOCUS YOU need by journaling.

Get the most out of your workbook. Write down your thoughts, insights, feelings, struggles, ideas, dreams, new concepts, plans/goals or anything that assists you.

Guaranteed Success Strategy #20:
Challenge Accepted

1. Have you ever been in a situation where your body was moving forward while your mind in apprehension was telling you, "No, stop?"

   _____
   _____
   _____
   _____

2. What was it that made you move past the point of passivity; what compelled you even while your knees were knocking?

   _____
   _____
   _____
   _____

3. Has there been a time when you were totally disappointed because you knew the moment called for more but you cowered down? Explain.

_____

_____

_____

_____

_____

4. On the other side of that regret what have you done to make sure you will stand tall when it's called for the next time?

_____

_____

_____

_____

_____

JOURNAL

Get the Life YOU Want and the FOCUS YOU need by journaling.

Get the most out of your workbook. Write down your thoughts, insights, feelings, struggles, ideas, dreams, new concepts, plans/goals or anything that assists you.

Guaranteed Success Strategy #21:
Make It Happen

1. The obstacles you think are holding you back from your dreams may not be as large as you think. What do you need to do in order to get pass your fears?

   _____
   _____
   _____
   _____
   _____

2. What initial step do you need to take in order to set things in motion?

   _____
   _____
   _____
   _____
   _____

3. "Apprehensions can cause paralysis when one simple act of courage can fuel your fire to great accomplishment." How has that played out in your life?

_____
_____
_____
_____
_____

4. Have you honestly sat down and planned out how you want the next couple years to go? What have you initiated in the plan?

_____
_____
_____
_____
_____

JOURNAL

Get the Life YOU Want and the FOCUS YOU need by journaling.

Get the most out of your workbook. Write down your thoughts, insights, feelings, struggles, ideas, dreams, new concepts, plans/goals or anything that assists you.

Guaranteed Success Strategy #22:
Show Up...TODAY

1. Yesterday didn't turn out the way you anticipated. Understood! But what keeps you from fully enveloping yourself into today?

   _____
   _____
   _____
   _____
   _____

2. Determined to, "Honor your worth." How do you do that?

   _____
   _____
   _____
   _____
   _____

3. Difficult situations and challenges can leave you winded and depleted. Take the time to reappraise your significance. Have you done that? What do you see?

_____
_____
_____
_____
_____

4. In assessing your worth, you have to give your all with no regrets associated with having held back. Can you do that?

_____
_____
_____
_____
_____

5. Stay WIDE – ALERT. How would that application work in your life?

_____
_____
_____

JOURNAL

Get the Life YOU Want and the FOCUS YOU need by journaling.

Get the most out of your workbook. Write down your thoughts, insights, feelings, struggles, ideas, dreams, new concepts, plans/goals or anything that assists you.

Guaranteed Success Strategy #23:
Be Professional

1. What practices have you put into place to separate personal biases from the professional arena?

_____
_____
_____
_____
_____

2. In the hiring process people aren't considered sometimes because of little things like the style of their hair. What are your thoughts on company specifications and job requirements when considering who you think would be best suited for a needed position?

_____
_____
_____
_____
_____

3. Discrimination in the work place and social settings is still very much a part of our climate though more subtle. What have you seen and how has it affected you?

_____

_____

_____

_____

_____

4. Have you achieved despite being unprofessional? Did it satisfy you and if so, how long?

_____

_____

_____

_____

_____

JOURNAL

Get the Life YOU Want and the FOCUS YOU need by journaling.

Get the most out of your workbook. Write down your thoughts, insights, feelings, struggles, ideas, dreams, new concepts, plans/goals or anything that assists you.

Now Work YOUR Plan:

| O | ▶ | **Own every opportunity** |

    A.   **FOCUS POINTS**

          _____

          _____

          _____

          _____

    B.   **CREATE YOUR STRATEGY**

          _____

          _____

          _____

          _____

    C.   **YOUR SPECIFIC 'DOABLE' TIMELINE**

          _____

          _____

          _____

          _____

FOCUS WORKBOOK & JOURNAL

foCus

Courage, Creativity, Caring = A Winning Combination

Guaranteed Success Strategy #24:
It's In There

Strengthen yourself by the words you speak and think.

1. How do you build yourself up?

   _____
   _____
   _____
   _____
   _____

2. Self-actualization requires your full involvement in your growth and development. What motivates you to make sure you reach your full potential?

   _____
   _____
   _____
   _____
   _____

3. Only you really know the public and private you. What do you have in place to make sure you're getting what you need to be at your best?

_____

_____

_____

_____

_____

JOURNAL

Get the Life YOU Want and the FOCUS YOU need by journaling.

Get the most out of your workbook. Write down your thoughts, insights, feelings, struggles, ideas, dreams, new concepts, plans/goals or anything that assists you.

Guaranteed Success Strategy #25:
Strength to Speak

1. Does fear keep you from speaking?

___

2. Which do you feel is the greater offense; not speaking or speaking and not being heard? Explain.

___

3. What would be at risk and to whom if you gathered the strength to speak?

4. "What you gain from the toughness it takes to speak opens you to the possibilities of what could be accomplished in so many areas of your life." Is that or is that not a true statement to you? Explain.

JOURNAL

Get the Life YOU Want and the FOCUS YOU need by journaling.

Get the most out of your workbook. Write down your thoughts, insights, feelings, struggles, ideas, dreams, new concepts, plans/goals or anything that assists you.

Guaranteed Success Strategy #26:
Start Believing

1. Why do you feel belief in yourself is such a critical part of success?

---

2. Are you secure with who you are in your current stage of life as far as your goals and professional vocation? Explain.

3. Much can be said about you good or bad to the point that you start believing what's being said. How do you separate what you hear from what you know?

_____

_____

_____

_____

4. "Our belief in ourselves needs to increase along with the demands of each endeavor." How can you make sure that happens?

_____

_____

_____

_____

5. Have you made positive changes since the last time things didn't work out as you imagined? How?

_____

_____

_____

JOURNAL

Get the Life YOU Want and the FOCUS YOU need by journaling.

Get the most out of your workbook. Write down your thoughts, insights, feelings, struggles, ideas, dreams, new concepts, plans/goals or anything that assists you.

_____

_____

_____

_____

_____

_____

_____

_____

_____

_____

_____

_____

_____

_____

_____

_____

Guaranteed Success Strategy #27:
Give It Time Please

Truth be told, there are no overnight successes; there were investments made along the way.
Consider your investments.

1. It takes time, discipline and patience to achieve the goals we set for our dreams and successes. Which have you had the most difficulty with – time, discipline, and/or patience? Why.

_____

_____

_____

_____

_____

2. The four key components: character, content, chemistry, and change will help you along the way. Which one do you need to focus on?

_____

_____

_____

_____

JOURNAL

Get the Life YOU Want and the FOCUS YOU need by journaling.

Get the most out of your workbook. Write down your thoughts, insights, feelings, struggles, ideas, dreams, new concepts, plans/goals or anything that assists you.

_____

_____

_____

_____

_____

_____

_____

_____

_____

_____

_____

_____

_____

_____

_____

_____

_____

Guaranteed Success Strategy #28:
Connecting the Dots

1. How do you translate what you've learned in theory to everyday practice?

2. How do you respond when the implementation of that theory leaves you at a loss?

3. What is your visualization and conceptualization process? Who do you trust for input?

_____

_____

_____

_____

_____

4. How far are you willing to go in making changes once you're finally able to connect the dots?

_____

_____

_____

_____

_____

JOURNAL

Get the Life YOU Want and the FOCUS YOU need by journaling.

Get the most out of your workbook. Write down your thoughts, insights, feelings, struggles, ideas, dreams, new concepts, plans/goals or anything that assists you.

Guaranteed Success Strategy #29:
Lysol or Scrubbing Bubbles

1. Do you find yourself doing what gives you life or are you just trudging along? Is major change in order? Explain.

2. Peace comes from understanding and being the best you that you can possibly be. Do you find yourself wanting to be something that you're totally incapable of being? How do you come to terms with knowing that your make-up is not suited for the direction you may be trying to go in?

3. You may not be a racehorse but you still have the tenacity of a frontrunner. How do you express yourself in accomplishing the challenge to find your flow?

_____
_____
_____
_____
_____

4. The diversity of our world is what makes for the beauty and success of it. How do you find ways to incorporate your gift into this diversity?

_____
_____
_____
_____
_____

5. What exactly are you here to do?

_____
_____
_____
_____

JOURNAL

Get the Life YOU Want and the FOCUS YOU need by journaling.

Get the most out of your workbook. Write down your thoughts, insights, feelings, struggles, ideas, dreams, new concepts, plans/goals or anything that assists you.

Guaranteed Success Strategy #30:
Change Direction

1. Are your ambitions too ambitious? If you answer yes, regroup. If you answer is no, is there anything keeping you from achieving them?

2. "Daily routines hold hostage individuals who die each day to what is expected of them as opposed to what breathes life into their being." Are you bound or free? Explain.

3. "There is no law in the universe that says you can't regroup, retool, change course, or go another way." What would it take to transform you or take you to the place you want to be?

_____

_____

_____

_____

_____

4. Your tenure in one place or fear of change is no longer a reason to maintain your present position when your heart longs for something else. You've exhausted all of the reasons why not to make that change. Now what?

_____

_____

_____

_____

_____

JOURNAL

Get the Life YOU Want and the FOCUS YOU need by journaling.

Get the most out of your workbook. Write down your thoughts, insights, feelings, struggles, ideas, dreams, new concepts, plans/goals or anything that assists you.

Guaranteed Success Strategy #31:
Make It Happen (Gut It Out)

1. It takes persistence and consistency to make it things happen. Are you putting these keys to work?

2. When you take complete ownership of your dreams you're not looking for someone else to make them come true. Have you given too much responsibility to someone else for the fulfillment of your dreams? Details.

3. Writing down your plan in working towards your desired end makes it more feasible and creditable. Have you written them down in a 'doable' format?

_____

_____

_____

_____

_____

4. You have what it takes to get it done; don't doubt that. Sometimes a major shift in mindsets is all it takes to get you on the road to your success. What's the biggest difference in how you think when productive versus when you're stuck?

_____

_____

_____

_____

_____

JOURNAL

Get the Life YOU Want and the FOCUS YOU need by journaling.

Get the most out of your workbook. Write down your thoughts, insights, feelings, struggles, ideas, dreams, new concepts, plans/goals or anything that assists you.

Guaranteed Success Strategy #32:
Be Flexible

1. Flexibility means doing the best you can with what you have at the time. Are you able to put this working definition of flexibility to work regardless of circumstances?

   _____
   _____
   _____
   _____
   _____

2. Not having what you thought you needed is no longer an acceptable excuse for not getting the job done. Do you look for an excuse or find hidden creativity in being flexible?

   _____
   _____
   _____
   _____
   _____

3. "Some people thrive off of a good challenge; others become paralyzed when faced with unexpected difficulties." How do you function?

_____

_____

_____

_____

_____

4. Flexibility can lighten the load of pressure we sometimes put upon ourselves wanting everything exactly as we think it should be. Have you found flexibility to be an asset or drawback? How so?

_____

_____

_____

_____

_____

JOURNAL

Get the Life YOU Want and the FOCUS YOU need by journaling.

Get the most out of your workbook. Write down your thoughts, insights, feelings, struggles, ideas, dreams, new concepts, plans/goals or anything that assists you.

Guaranteed Success Strategy #33:
Is It Real or Not?

1. "Rightness is anchored by truth and truth doesn't change given the environment or the climate." What kind of challenges have you faced when refusing to change the truth?

   _____

   _____

   _____

   _____

2. As an individual how do you contribute to the value of speaking and exchanging in an open and straightforward manner?

   _____

   _____

   _____

   _____

JOURNAL

Get the Life YOU Want and the FOCUS YOU need by journaling.

Get the most out of your workbook. Write down your thoughts, insights, feelings, struggles, ideas, dreams, new concepts, plans/goals or anything that assists you.

Now Work YOUR Plan:

| C | ▶ | Courage, creativity & caring = a winning combination |

    A.   **FOCUS POINTS**

           _____

           _____

           _____

           _____

    B.   **CREATE YOUR STRATEGY**

           _____

           _____

           _____

           _____

    C.   **YOUR SPECIFIC 'DOABLE' TIMELINE**

           _____

           _____

           _____

           _____

FOCUS WORKBOOK & JOURNAL

focUs

YOU REALLY DO MATTER

Guaranteed Success Strategy #34:
Here's To You

1. "Facing the facts is empowering while ignoring them is debilitating." Which has been the case for you? Explain.

   _____
   _____
   _____
   _____
   _____

2. Wise management assesses the problem and brings in expert help if necessary. Would you characterize yourself as shrewd and astute or one who continually repeats the same mistakes yielding the same results? Details.

   _____
   _____
   _____
   _____
   _____

3. Growth is indicated when you come to the reality that you can't do it alone and benefit from the help of others. What was the process that made this real for you?

_____

_____

_____

_____

_____

JOURNAL

Get the Life YOU Want and the FOCUS YOU need by journaling.

Get the most out of your workbook. Write down your thoughts, insights, feelings, struggles, ideas, dreams, new concepts, plans/goals or anything that assists you.

Guaranteed Success Strategy #35:
Not Perfection but Progress

1. Understanding the enlightened meaning of perfection, how do you measure yourself?

   _____
   _____
   _____
   _____
   _____

2. If you make progress but miss the mark of perfection what enables you to move forward whatever the conclusion?

   _____
   _____
   _____
   _____
   _____

3. "Don't fall apart when you fall short, recover…" How do you embrace that statement?

_____

_____

_____

_____

_____

4. "I am flawed and have faults but I'm working on a daily version of *better*." Are you willing and able to grow that "better" into perfection (maturity)? How, or why not?

_____

_____

_____

_____

_____

JOURNAL

Get the Life YOU Want and the FOCUS YOU need by journaling.

Get the most out of your workbook. Write down your thoughts, insights, feelings, struggles, ideas, dreams, new concepts, plans/goals or anything that assists you.

_____

_____

_____

_____

_____

_____

_____

_____

_____

_____

_____

_____

_____

_____

_____

_____

_____

Guaranteed Success Strategy #36:
Relationship Practices *That Really Work*!

1. In Relationship Practice #1, how can you be a better listener?

   _____

   _____

   _____

   _____

   _____

2. Communication is an absolute necessity in relationships. Are you hindered or willing to talk? What is your approach to discussing problems?

   _____

   _____

   _____

   _____

   _____

3. Controlling your anger and of course apologizing is critical. *"It garners respect and trust in a way that nothing else will."* Should your need to grow your business and personal relationships be bigger than your individual image? Yes or no, explain.

_____

_____

_____

_____

_____

4. Keeping every practice in mind, how will you make them work in your right now?

_____

_____

_____

_____

_____

JOURNAL

Get the Life YOU Want and the FOCUS YOU need by journaling.

Get the most out of your workbook. Write down your thoughts, insights, feelings, struggles, ideas, dreams, new concepts, plans/goals or anything that assists you.

_____

_____

_____

_____

_____

_____

_____

_____

_____

_____

_____

_____

_____

_____

_____

_____

Guaranteed Success Strategy #37:
The Ever Evolving You

1. What is your reaction to change?

2. Besides present conditions being familiar and manageable, from your perspective, why is change met with resistance?

3. There can be a sadness in not taking a chance, changing, and going for what you want. What would be of greater detriment to you, staying where you are or taking that chance? Why?

_____

_____

_____

_____

_____

4. If you did make a significant change, describe your experience.

_____

_____

_____

_____

_____

JOURNAL

Get the Life YOU Want and the FOCUS YOU need by journaling.

Get the most out of your workbook. Write down your thoughts, insights, feelings, struggles, ideas, dreams, new concepts, plans/goals or anything that assists you.

Guaranteed Success Strategy #38:
Chaos Needs No Accommodation

1. The term 'Controlled Chaos' is contradictory but has become an expression widely used in today's society. What does it mean to you?

   _____

   _____

   _____

   _____

   _____

2. If you take a closer look at the environment, you can see that the chaos is not controlled and so many are suffering because there are no boundaries and things have gotten out of hand. When you're in recognition of the real chaos, do you go along or find productive ways to share your concern/make changes?

   _____

   _____

   _____

   _____

   _____

3. The absence of order can account for you being drained, frustrated and ticked off; trying to put a square peg into a round hole. Things are taking a toll on you. How do you keep yourself from suffering the impact of disorder?

_____

_____

_____

_____

_____

4. How do you position yourself for streaming success and nothing else?

_____

_____

_____

_____

_____

JOURNAL

Get the Life YOU Want and the FOCUS YOU need by journaling.

Get the most out of your workbook. Write down your thoughts, insights, feelings, struggles, ideas, dreams, new concepts, plans/goals or anything that assists you.

Guaranteed Success Strategy #39:
You Eat With Your Eyes First

1. You've already started the process of expectation. What hope/dream/career/goal are you eating now?

   _____
   _____
   _____
   _____

2. Or…are you at a dead end not experiencing the consumption of what it is you want so badly in life? What's your next move to get you close?

   _____
   _____
   _____
   _____

JOURNAL

Get the Life YOU Want and the FOCUS YOU need by journaling.

Get the most out of your workbook. Write down your thoughts, insights, feelings, struggles, ideas, dreams, new concepts, plans/goals or anything that assists you.

Guaranteed Success Strategy #40:
The Difference Maker

1. What motivates you?

   _____

   _____

   _____

   _____

   _____

2. How has your support system influenced you?

   _____

   _____

   _____

   _____

   _____

3. Do you recognize varying forms of help and what it's intended to provide?

___

4. How do you express to your support system your thanks for them being there?

___

JOURNAL

Get the Life YOU Want and the FOCUS YOU need by journaling.

Get the most out of your workbook. Write down your thoughts, insights, feelings, struggles, ideas, dreams, new concepts, plans/goals or anything that assists you.

Guaranteed Success Strategy #41:
Investment Translates into Ownership

1. Whatever stage you're in, it's important to know you do matter. But what happens when you're in situations and associations where you're not acknowledged; how do you handle it?

2. "Each time you show up, it's an investment and the sharper you are the more valuable your investment becomes." The more you give you, the more you are devoted and the greater the feeling of ownership. How do you take care of what *belongs to you*?

3. Do you own the results of your investment?

_____

_____

_____

_____

_____

4. Knowing the results wouldn't have been what they were had you not been invested; what type of satisfaction do you get in knowing the desired end was realized because of your investment?

_____

_____

_____

_____

_____

JOURNAL

Get the Life YOU Want and the FOCUS YOU need by journaling.

Get the most out of your workbook. Write down your thoughts, insights, feelings, struggles, ideas, dreams, new concepts, plans/goals or anything that assists you.

_____

_____

_____

_____

_____

_____

_____

_____

_____

_____

_____

_____

_____

_____

_____

Guaranteed Success Strategy #42:
A Heart to Come Home To

1. Is your home a place of relaxation, rejuvenation and safety for you?

   _____
   _____
   _____
   _____
   _____

2. Does your heart have a place to go for comfort, joy and rest?

   _____
   _____
   _____
   _____
   _____

3. Have you taken the time to build the foundations of a quality life with people that matter to you?

_____
_____
_____
_____
_____

4. Are you secure within yourself which will enhance how you share with those that matter most to you? In a healthy way, how do you make yourself a priority to continue your secure state?

_____
_____
_____
_____
_____

It's all about the satisfaction found in a meaningful existence. Remember, YOU DO MATTER!

JOURNAL

Get the Life YOU Want and the FOCUS YOU need by journaling.

Get the most out of your workbook. Write down your thoughts, insights, feelings, struggles, ideas, dreams, new concepts, plans/goals or anything that assists you.

Now Work YOUR Plan:

| U | ▶ | U *really* do matter |

    A.   **FOCUS POINTS**

              _____

              _____

              _____

              _____

    B.   **CREATE YOUR STRATEGY**

              _____

              _____

              _____

              _____

    C.   **YOUR SPECIFIC 'DOABLE' TIMELINE**

              _____

              _____

              _____

              _____

FOCUS Workbook & Journal

FOCUS

Success as a Way of Life

Guaranteed Success Strategy #43:
A Good Loss

1. Revisit your last defeat. Look at it from a different perspective. What can you see now that you weren't able to see before?

   _____
   _____
   _____
   _____
   _____

2. Although your loss was disappointing, how has your focus and determination been heightened by the total experience?

   _____
   _____
   _____
   _____
   _____

3. "To some degree I don't even mind losing anymore, I call it *practice*." Practice is where you get repetitions until you get it right. Is this a philosophy you embrace? Explain.

_____

_____

_____

_____

JOURNAL

Get the Life YOU Want and the FOCUS YOU need by journaling.

Get the most out of your workbook. Write down your thoughts, insights, feelings, struggles, ideas, dreams, new concepts, plans/goals or anything that assists you.

Guaranteed Success Strategy #44:
Do a Good Day's *Work* *and* Act Like Somebody

1. "Your work ethic says everything about you." What is yours saying?

2. Most successful people were not loafers on those jobs that had nothing to do with their ultimate goal career-wise. But those jobs became character builders and proven ground for good work practices. What did you gain from workplaces that were just 'a job' to you?

3. "While it is that people don't have to like you…you do want them to respect you and not hate the sight of you." Respected or disrespected; what has your workplace behavior garnered?

_____

_____

_____

_____

_____

JOURNAL

Get the Life YOU Want and the FOCUS YOU need by journaling.

Get the most out of your workbook. Write down your thoughts, insights, feelings, struggles, ideas, dreams, new concepts, plans/goals or anything that assists you.

Guaranteed Success Strategy #45:
Only the Best Will Do

1. Do you give your best without fail?

2. Giving your best is reflective of who you are at that point. "A best you is yet waiting to emerge." How do you keep yourself open and primed for the greatness of who you can become?

3. Are you able to readily see things now that can positively / negatively feed into the foundational you? How do you properly address them?

JOURNAL

Get the Life YOU Want and the FOCUS YOU need by journaling.

Get the most out of your workbook. Write down your thoughts, insights, feelings, struggles, ideas, dreams, new concepts, plans/goals or anything that assists you.

Guaranteed Success Strategy #46:
Unmistakably You

1. What distinctive impact do you have in your sphere?

   _____
   _____
   _____
   _____
   _____

2. Do you fully engage yourself regardless the situation, task, or environment? What do you do to make sure you're fully connected?

   _____
   _____
   _____
   _____
   _____

3. Does your involvement lend itself to better or worse outcome? Explain.

_____

_____

_____

_____

_____

4. As things stand now, if you were mentoring someone, what would you want them to take aware from their dynamic with you?

_____

_____

_____

_____

_____

JOURNAL

Get the Life YOU Want and the FOCUS YOU need by journaling.

Get the most out of your workbook. Write down your thoughts, insights, feelings, struggles, ideas, dreams, new concepts, plans/goals or anything that assists you.

Guaranteed Success Strategy #47:
Play Your Game but Always Be Ready

1. Bring the best you to the table and at the same time respect the game, job, position, etc. How do you do that?

   _____
   _____
   _____
   _____
   _____

2. The variable that you control in the equation is, YOU. How do you make that variable work optimally?

   _____
   _____
   _____
   _____
   _____

3. Keep your head in the moment, that's part of mastering it and respecting it. If mentally, you're all over the place – you're already defeated. How do you respect what's called for in the 'right now?'

_____
_____
_____
_____
_____

4. How do you get ready and stay ready especially when you don't know when the 'ready' time will come?

_____
_____
_____
_____
_____

JOURNAL

Get the Life YOU Want and the FOCUS YOU need by journaling.

Get the most out of your workbook. Write down your thoughts, insights, feelings, struggles, ideas, dreams, new concepts, plans/goals or anything that assists you.

_____

_____

_____

_____

_____

_____

_____

_____

_____

_____

_____

_____

_____

_____

_____

_____

Guaranteed Success Strategy #48:
!!?Can You Recognize It?!!

1. What does success look like to you?

   _____

   _____

   _____

   _____

   _____

2. How do you measure it?

   _____

   _____

   _____

   _____

   _____

3. What are the intangibles?

_____

_____

_____

_____

4. Whatever is most important to you will be what's most prevalently out front, speaking to, and representing who you are. What does your reflection say about you?

_____

_____

_____

_____

5. How will success look on YOU?

_____

_____

_____

_____

JOURNAL

Get the Life YOU Want and the FOCUS YOU need by journaling.

Get the most out of your workbook. Write down your thoughts, insights, feelings, struggles, ideas, dreams, new concepts, plans/goals or anything that assists you.

Guaranteed Success Strategy #49:
Leadership

1. Are you a leader? What makes you a leader or prohibits you from being a leader?

_____
_____
_____
_____
_____

2. In the leaders you've encounter what qualities stood out to you that made them good/bad leaders?

_____
_____
_____
_____
_____

3. Becoming that person in the forefront requires that you not be afraid of failure but embrace the knowledge in the experience gained." What knowledge have you gained from an experience that didn't have the results you expected?

_____

_____

_____

_____

_____

4. Besides personal dynamics, leadership is encompassed with knowledge and skills. If you were mentoring someone for a leadership role, what would you pass on to them?

_____

_____

_____

_____

_____

JOURNAL

Get the Life YOU Want and the FOCUS YOU need by journaling.

Get the most out of your workbook. Write down your thoughts, insights, feelings, struggles, ideas, dreams, new concepts, plans/goals or anything that assists you.

Guaranteed Success Strategy #50:
Sharpened Image, Refined Goods

1. What is it that you bring to the table that differentiates you and sets you apart from everybody else?

   _____

   _____

   _____

   _____

   _____

2. Does your business offerings make your clientele prefer you over others? Your product? Customer service you render? Explain.

   _____

   _____

   _____

   _____

   _____

3. For whatever business or services you render you must "lock in on what you want to present, and do it well." How would your clients rate or grade the business / service you render to them? How often to you ask for their valued input?

_____
_____
_____
_____
_____

4. Do you present beautiful or sharp aesthetics to your clients / customers?

_____
_____
_____
_____
_____

JOURNAL

Get the Life YOU Want and the FOCUS YOU need by journaling.

Get the most out of your workbook. Write down your thoughts, insights, feelings, struggles, ideas, dreams, new concepts, plans/goals or anything that assists you.

Guaranteed Success Strategy #51: **Pass It On**

1. The most important things in life can't be bought. We know that, we've heard it a million times. What intangible can you give to someone else that would make a world of difference in their life?

2. Society as a whole has lost so much because we've come to recognizing only those things that superficially make us look better and seem better. What makes you the person that you are and would you want to be emulated?

3. Most times we're on our best behavior around children because they are imitators. In just being you, what would someone see just hanging out with you for a day? Would you be proud or disappointed in you?

_____

_____

_____

_____

_____

4. "We don't have to stand by and continue to allow things to spiral. We can save the generations to come by passing on a quality of life." Do you showcase that quality without ever having to speak?

_____

_____

_____

_____

_____

JOURNAL

Get the Life YOU Want and the FOCUS YOU need by journaling.

Get the most out of your workbook. Write down your thoughts, insights, feelings, struggles, ideas, dreams, new concepts, plans/goals or anything that assists you.

Guaranteed Success Strategy #52:
Wow, Keep It Coming

1. We're measured by what we do over and over again. Are others excited or have no expectancy by what you bring? Explain why.

   _____

   _____

   _____

   _____

   _____

2. Consistency speaks well of us. "Look to make your course regular, that men may know beforehand what they may expect." Is your course consistent?

   _____

   _____

   _____

   _____

   _____

Now Work YOUR Plan:

| S | ▶ | **Success as a way of life** |

    A.   **FOCUS POINTS**

           _____

           _____

           _____

           _____

    B.   **CREATE YOUR STRATEGY**

           _____

           _____

           _____

           _____

    C.   **YOUR SPECIFIC 'DOABLE' TIMELINE**

           _____

           _____

           _____

           _____

When you're consistently FOCUSED, and allow your brilliance to operate fully; *you will*
Get the LIFE YOU WANT!

Enjoy and Live EXPECTANTLY!...

Made in the USA
Middletown, DE
05 February 2017